GW00542491

LIFE LINES

poetry *Pt* today

LIFE LINES

Edited by
Rebecca Mee

First published in Great Britain in 1998 by Poetry
Today, an imprint of
Penhaligon Page Ltd, 12 Godric Square, Maxwell Road,
Peterborough. PE2 7JJ

© Copyright Contributors 1998

All rights reserved. No part of this publication may be
reproduced, stored in a retrieval system, or transmitted
in any form or by any means, without prior permission
from the author(s).

A Catalogue record for this book is available from the
British Library

ISBN 1 86226 099 0

Typesetting and layout, Penhaligon Page Ltd, England.
Printed and bound by Forward Press Ltd, England

Foreword

Life Lines is a compilation of poetry, featuring some
of our finest poets. The book gives an insight into
the essence of modern living and deals with the
reality of life today. We think we have created an
anthology with a universal appeal.

There are many technical aspects to the writing of
poetry and *Life Lines* contains free verse and
examples of more structured work from a wealth of
talented poets.

Poetry is a coat of many colours. Today's poets write
in a limitless array of styles: traditional rhyming
poetry is as alive and kicking today as modern free-
verse. Language ranges from easily accessible to
intricate and elusive.

Poems have a lot to offer in our fast-paced 'instant'
world. Reading poems gives us an opportunity to sit
back and explore ourselves and the world around
us.

Contents

Tiny Little Lady

Tiny little lady much wisdom in small head.
Never be diverted, her special path would tread.
Working hard each day to help her family.
Washing, cleaning, cooking, she kept the home debt free.

To educate her sons great sacrifices made.
In partnership with husband 'til he went to his grave.
He, hard working miner, in dank and narrow pit.
Cramped in bad conditions, with pick the coal would split.

They went to church each Sunday; it was the Christian way.
One son had music lessons 'til organ he could play.
War came to the country, serviceman lads were made.
In years they did their duty, parents much pride displayed.

When the war was over these two lads got wed.
Parents were delighted at paths both sons did tread.
Then tiny little lady lost her husband dear.
Though now up in heaven, always she felt him near.

Her sons she let live their lives, she lived out her own.
Both would come to visit from where they dwelled in town.
First son's wife died of illness, so after time had gone.
He wedded a sweet new maid, and life just carried on.

Tiny little lady still clever as could be,
Shared home with friend of some years, leaving both sons free.
Knowing in her wisdom, strong are chains of love.
Keeping her lads in contact 'til she joined dad above.

Lord spared her many long years to live upon this earth.
Her honesty and goodness showed all her special worth.
Of money she had little, so must live frugally
But was the richest lady of all folk known by me.

Barbara Goode

Card-iology

A little boy David, aged four, I knew well,
Played cards with our neighbour, before he could spell!
Knew the number of cards contained in a pack,
The court cards name, and could shuffle and stack.

At aged five, this young man on his first day at school,
Thought counting a subject he'd handle real cool!
His response was immediate when teacher said then,
'Hands up anyone who can count beyond ten.'

David said, 'I can Miss,' and unhesitating,
He counted to ten, adding Jack, queen & king
Highly tickled, his teacher, with kindly regards,
That day taught him numbers that weren't on the cards!

Marcia Elizabeth Jenkin

Cornish Gardens

Gardens have something to offer
All seasons of the year.
Cornwall boasts some famous ones,
That is very clear.
If gardening skills you wish to learn
To pick up information
Then, Probus is the one for you -
Just watch their demonstration.

While Heligan has everything,
So many sights to see,
From shrubs and flowers and rockeries
And every kind of tree . . .
Kitchen gardens, lawns and walks,
Even a wishing well,
Exotic plants and tempting fruit,
And many a charming dell.

But if you wish to venture
A few miles out to sea,
To the lovely Isle of Tresco
Enchanting things you'll see.
In the famous Abbey Gardens,
Protected from the gales
By the massive holm oak hedges,
So that warmth within prevails.

In spring and early summer,
Trebah Garden is the best,
With gigantic rhododendrons,
The finest in the west.
And blue and white hydrangeas
Leading downward to the shore,
A Cornish panorama,
And who could ask for more?

Kathleen Earle

4

Fun On November The Fifth

It's Bangers tonight, and Sparklers - all right?
I enjoy a good fireworks show.
There might be a Rocket, if there's cash in Dad's pocket;
But 'Dog eared' the cat will not go.

There'll be Candles and stuff; and ones which go 'puff';
There'll be bright coloured showers of light.
But Dad says, 'Be good: now is that understood?
Or you won't even go out tonight.'

Then after the fire, we will nearly expire;
But Mum has a treat still in store:
There'll be litres of Pop, with bubbles on top;
Baked potatoes with cheese, and much more.

So if I take care, all my friends will be there;
We'll remember what has to be done.
We will offer our thanks; and ensure there's no pranks;
So the fifth of November is fun.

David J Workman

Reflections

I see many faces through the day -
All passing on their busy way -
The happy face - or one of sadness -
That hat perched high in utter madness -
The older face with parchment skin -
Or cheeky youth - with teenage grin -
I'll show them what they want to see -
When preening - oh what vanity -
You'll find me daily used by all -
For I'm the 'mirror' on the wall.

Anna Edwards

Grandparents

Grandparents are special and
They only come but once,
Have you heard the story of
How they first meet.
It was oh so long ago and the
Years have passed.
But their love grows ever
Like a rose.

No day has passed with out
A thought about the other
One,
The road to ever lasting love
Is never quite so smooth,
You are still beautiful, granddad
Tells us so.
He holds a candle bright
For thee always to be true.

Marie Dorrian

Spring

Oh! spring is here. Oh! spring is here,
   And now the world is glad
For flowers, and beasts and birds are near;
   The trees with leaves are clad.
The cuckoo's voice is heard once more
   Within the woods so green.
He sings from his hearts very core
   Although he is not seen.
And now that April's come and gone
   Sweet May is here again.
'Tis during May, when work is done
   We sing an old refrain.
Ah! spring is here. Ah! spring is here.
   The lanes are strewn with flowers,
While bees and flies hum everywhere
   Between the sunny showers.

Christine J Raymer

A Mild November

Summer lingers still, reluctant to leave us.
A bright orange poppy head, Oriental variety, in full bloom.

One solitary sunflower, though short in stem 'tis true,
Turns its golden yellow head, towards the low noonday sun.

Even the Doris pink, dainty as a ballerina,
Pleases us with sweet late blooms, and brightens up the border.

The rosebuds open out, with the same fragrant blush,
As they did in early summer! But it is now mid-autumn!

Purple lavender spikes, delight, as do bright pansies.
The hanging fuchsias blooms, vie with pink geranium heads.

Even, late in season, red raspberries, ripe for picking!
Lush green grass grows round our feet, dotted with tawny toadstools.

Did no-one tell them? It is November now.
The time of chill mists and frosts; and fallen, golden, trampled
leaves.

May our November days, be blessed with touch of summer;
May the autumn of our lives, be full of warm, bright memories.

Mary Rowe

Reflections Of An 80 Year Old

Now that my days are less busy
And I have more time on my hands.
I sit in my chair and write letters
And spend time in thought with my friends.

I remind them of days spent together,
Of holidays down by the sea,
Of fun with our children when they were all small
And we swam and climbed mountains so free.

I know that my letters are welcomed
As I soon get a cheerful reply.
And I feel that my friends though so far away
Could almost be living nearby.

So I'll carry on writing my letters
While I still have something to share,
Though I'm no longer bodily active
I can write from my old armchair.

Kathleen Pike

Trapped In The Tower

I'm trapped in the tower alone, just now,
But soon the big bell will strike.
The cogs will turn and the hammer will swing.
The bell will go ding, dong, ding.
On and on the hands of time go,
Never too fast never too slow.
The rushing people go along,
But stop when they hear the bell song.
I see children, mums and all sorts of men,
Here alone in the tower of Big Ben.

Andrew Fishman

Dad

All through his working life, my Dad,
Worked down the pit, no light he had.
Deep in the bowels of the earth,
Sweating and toiling, for all he was worth.
He's retired today, I'm so happy to say.
But the legacy will never go away.
The reward is the dust, all miners will know,
That sticks to their lungs, never to go.
I for one, am so very glad,
He survived it in one piece, did my Dad.
He'd wake up at dawn, since before I was born,
To toil in the pit, that was so poorly lit.
Out the front way, each and every day
I knew when his bus came, from my bed
Because I couldn't here his coughing, in my head.
Such a dangerous job, for just a few bob.
Accidents that he has seen,
But for grace,
Could he have been.
When your Dad is a miner, so soon your to learn
That there's no guarantee, that he will return
He's had his share of lucky misses,
I had my share of my father's kisses.
Lots of kids not so lucky as me,
A life without Dad, their fated to see.
Gone is the child that worries, and sits,
And so glad to say,
Gone too are the pits.
I'm happy and glad, to still have my Dad.
For my life, I'm very grateful, I know I'm right to say,
We were very very lucky, Dad you came home each day.

Angela Richards

My Grandad

He doesn't like Quiche and he doesn't like Flan,
But he will tell you all about the hosepipe ban.

He stays in his greenhouse all day long,
Planting his seeds, and whistling a song.

He's always got Simba (the cat) by his side,
Who chases the farm cats and makes them hide.

He likes the News on TV with a cigar and a cup of tea.
When I'm naughty it's oh! dear oh! and off up the garden he will go.

I Love my Grandad, he's cool, he's great,
And he'll always be, My best Mate.

Yasmin Lucy Heathfield

Pops

You were there to pick me up
Whenever I should fall
And you were there to answer me
Whenever I should call
You were there to point the way
Whenever I was lost
In life's confusing labyrinth
You were someone I could trust

I hope that you were proud of me
As I am proud of you.
I still can hear your quoting words
In everything I do
So many treasured memories
Of you acting the fool
To pick me up when I was down
When life was being cruel

Of kicking footballs in the park
And playing hide and seek
Those peek-a-boos and dirty shoes
Still haunt me in my sleep
Letting me watch TV.
When I should have gone to bed
But Eric and Ernie made us laugh
With the things they did and said

And listening to 'old blue eyes'
Singing strangers in the night
Was my first taste of music
And my ears filled with delight
I wish that it was possible
To say these words to you
Of telling you I love you
And wond'rin' if you knew

So Pops if you are listening
And watching me tonight
I thank you for my memories
For teaching wrong from right
And when my son asks me
The questions I once asked of you
I'll answer with all honesty
The way you used to do

And hope to guide him
With the love and care you gave to me
And that my memories of you
Will be your legacy.

J Hogan

A Mother's Love

There is no love on this whole earth
then the love of your own mother,
she is every bit her worth
and you should always love her.

As you went through your childhood years,
she kept you free from harm,
with all your tantrums and your tears
she still held you in her arms.

Even through your teenage years,
when times were pretty hard,
she'd see you through your difficult times
and send you loving cards.

Then when you became adult,
and decided to fly the nest,
did she sit at home and sulk?
no she wished you all the best.

So next time you see your mother,
tell her you love her dear,
you may not get another time,
so tell her while she's here.

   Kathleen Tutty

Diana's Farewell

'Oh! Diana, can you see
All your people, there to be
At your passing, journeys end
From our sight, to on its wend
To your final resting place
Travelling at its funeral pace.
Not so long ago you went
To your wedding, which was rent
With deep sorrow not to be
A fairy tale for us to see.
'I vow to thee my country' said;
Many tears that then were shed,
But you rose above your grief
Bringing love, and so relief
To the many filled by stress
Shared with all, by our Princess.
You touched all hearts, as was your wish
By holding hands, a hug, a kiss
And finally it reached us here
To love, is how to cast out fear.
A love that blossomed at your end
Which broke your body, not to mend
You entered through the heavenly gate
With Dodi, in eternal state.
Happiness to there fulfil
God's own presence, and His will.
We will not forget you ever
And with deeds, will so endeavour
To give our love throughout this world
That you have proved in life, unfurled
Status matters not at all
Only love we can install
Learn our lessons in our life
Meant to set us free, from strife.
Love and cherish all we can
To our every fellow man.

And so this life is ended here
With love so echoed loud and clear
God enfold you close for ever
Which no sorrow now can sever.'

Marjorie Mann

The New Dawn

As I open my curtains on this new dawn
I see the sun rise like an orange balloon
Chasing night shadows away off the lawn
Giving way to the dew glistening and fresh
Birds singing, flying, looking for food
Soon they'll be feeding another new brood
Daffodils yellow waving about in the breeze
Promising more yet to come, of colour and splendour is springtime
sun

After winters harsh conditions of ice and snow
It's a miracle that anything survives
Next will be summer with picnics outside
Amid buttercups and daisies and all the hayrides
So look forward with gladness on this new dawn
And give thanks for the harvest
Of seeds that are sown.

Joyce Shakesby

The Magical Pond

The woodland is silent apart from the trees
Gently rustling in the early summer breeze.
Deep in these woods, through the birches beyond,
Is a secret place hiding a magical pond.
Watch carefully, with patience, and it never fails
To reveal wondrous secrets as its magic unveils.
This enchanting pond is really quite small
And all seems so quiet, but wait - that's the call
Of a little green frog who is sitting upon
His lily leaf lookout, then 'plop', he has gone.
Beneath gently rippling water frogs offspring abound,
Still tadpoles, their bodies rotund, black and round,
Tails are now shrinking, legs growing strong.
Miniature frogs will emerge before long.
Look closely at the surface - not just a glance,
See pond skaters gleefully dancing their dance.
A water spider surfaces, watch as he drags
Down a fresh silvery airbell beneath yellow iris flags.
Through ivy leafed duckweed, water boatman row,
Whilst flatworm and leeches are busy below.
Great diving beetles, nymphs of mayfly,
Newts, toads and snails, with luck you may spy.
Dragonfly and damselfly, overlooking these scenes,
Add exquisite beauty through reds, blues and greens.
Some may glance briefly but be unaware
Of the myriad of wonders which you have found, there
Deep in the woods, through the birches beyond,
In the secret place hiding this magical pond.

L A Norman

Roller Coaster

It will not stop taking me for the ride of my life.
Taking me up one minute, then down the next.
Going around and around, flinging me from one side to the other.
Then dangling me upside down, twisting and turning at full speed.
So thrilling yet also terrifying.
The feeling of dread becomes over ruled by excitement.
It feels like being on top of the world,
as I look down at the scenery all around me.
Before plunging down, down into the depths of mixed emotions.
Fear, excitement, enjoyment to stomach churning dislike.
It rolls on and on until I just want it to stop.
I'm feeling queasy as it slows down before drawing to a halt.
Getting off and all I can think about, is going on it again?

Lynn Kilpatrick

Mother's Tears

There are many of us in life, whose Mother's words are
                                                        lightly thought
                                                                upon.
But how they come back to us, the minute she's dead and gone.
Oh, Lord please overlook discretions, which I have slipped aside.
For the man's not bone, we are erstwhile, remember Eastertide.

It's dream of Fame and Fortune that lures us far and wide,
a mystery we need to fathom out, for our future and our pride.
This need to dream and build castles in the air,
is a carefree youthful heart, one's guilt we will not declare.

There are times in memory, I see the cosy home,
the memory of the hearth, its teapot of polished chrome.
The tears that were in Mother's eyes, her heart within her voice.
Oh, Mother, love of mine, you gave such good advice.

Now there's a great amount of water, run under the bridge of life.
I still remember the greatest piece told me by my Mother,
                                        as she held
                                        bread and knife.
Listen Lad, you'll promise - 'if you've tousled all your hair'.
You'll not forget, hang down your head - remember -
                                                'The Lord's Prayer'.

Alan Noble

Healing Wings

Suddenly my heart takes 'wings'
And soars to heights unknown,
My spirit lifts me up and up
To a far-off place I'm borne.

I know not why, I know not where
I feel so silent and so stilled,
The peace without, the peace within
My whole being is utterly filled.

It is a tranquil beauty rare
It is a silent powerful prayer.
'Tis too sacred for words to speak
It is the true divine, laid bare.

These moments of such silence
Seem to linger into hours,
The soul is so entranced hereby
That nothing else empowers.

The 'wings' that lift the heart so high
That help the spirit to soar,
To worlds of beauty, worlds of love
Which help, which heal, which endure.

These 'healing wings' are ever there
To help the soul take flight,
So reach upwards to that great peace
And soar into the light.

William Price

Untitled
(Dedicated to my loving Mother,
by her loving son James)

This is a poem about my Mother
Kind and loving like no other,
She drives us crazy with poems galore
But so fine they are we daren't ignore.

When it comes to kindness
She can't be beat, the opposition
Fall at her feet.

Her life's been hard
Till this day, she still asks God
To help her on her way,
As life these days seem ever so sad
The way peoples opinions seem so mad.

Her baking is ever so good, as
She makes such quality food,
The poems she writes ooze such class
But modesty she says 'they will pass'.

Words can't say, all that she means to us today
Please don't ever go away in our hearts you
Will always stay.

Love James

Dedicated to my loving Mother

Margaret Ramsey

Grand Parents

Here are my feelings for two people so dear,
To let them know they are loved throughout the year,
Two people so special and I will make them see,
How very much they both mean to me.

The 'people' I refer to if you haven't already guessed,
They are my Nan & Grandad and they simply are the best,
I can truly say without a doubt that they have always shown,
A little girl the way to go that she would never have known.

Nan and Grandad you are both so fine,
I am really glad I can say you are mine,
You are loving, caring and so giving too,
I have so many reasons to repay you.

My childhood memories with you are so great,
They begin with our pet dog - Dougal - my mate!
You made your house so welcome and invited me to stay,
A bedroom to call my own but 'keep it tidy' you would say.

To play with friends was just not me,
In the garden with Grandad was the best place to be,
I watched him in his shed to see how things were done,
Then wrote my name in his cement - oh we had so much fun!

While in the kitchen Nan would be,
Then she would shout 'come in for tea!'
Now wash your hands that is a must,
Eat all your food including your crust!

Each Friday night we would depart,
To a caravan I loved with all my heart,
We had many good times in Walton-on-naze,
Where on the beach we would laze.

The trips to Germany they were fun too,
Nan twiddling her thumbs - working out the miles we would do,
Grandad would sit there quiet and sweet,
With Nan always telling him to sit up and be neat.

Words cannot explain how much you mean to me,
If it wasn't for you then where would I be?
You have taught me everything from right and wrong,
Knowledge, manners, respect - the list is so long.

Through times good and bad you have always been there,
To hug me, love me and show that you care,
When I did well you have given me praise,
This meant so much on those special days.

To share my life with Grandparents like you,
Has been such an honour and that is so true,
So there's one last thing that I must say,
I Love You Both more every single day.

Lisa Boorman

Fields Of Childhood

What lovely things we used to do! Our childish days would bring
Bright minutes hung like daisies on the chains we used to string;
With time to lie in scented grass on drowsy afternoons
Of honeybee and butterfly through endless sunny Junes.

And once we took the local train - it must have been in May -
To meet my father, visiting-oh, many miles away,
I cannot tell how many, was it five, perhaps or ten?-
A village deep in cowslip fields, remote from traffic then.

Was it only through one summer that, responsible at eight,
We would daily fetch the cattle that were gathered at the gate?
For half a mile, unhurriedly, we sauntered in their track
To the farmyard and the milking shed, then rode the horses back.

As soon as school was over and the tea was cleared away,
Came Margaret or Leslie to the door with, 'Can you play?'
And rainy day or snowy day, whatever might befall,
There were so many things to do, no day could hold them all.

With see-saw and with shuttlecock, with kite and skipping-rope,
With hopscotch and with 'Let's pretend' reflecting childish hope -
An ordered pattern, stable, safe, with old things ever new -
Do children now have time to spare for all we used to do?

Kathleen M Hatton

The Chosen Soul

My heart is pierced and full of sorrow
I weep for those with no tomorrow.
Children scream in their mothers womb
Satanic surgery ensures their doom.

Poor little souls in a limbo state
Baptismal rites would mean they're safe.
Innocent martyrs cry out to the Lord
The Angel of Wrath shall wield his sword.

Low animal lust in the human condition
Gomorra and Sodom shall face perdition.
Faster than light his wrath shall come
Destruction for all who abandoned his son.

Many shall scoff at these written words
No place for such in the humanist world.
Their fear shall come when they least expect
He will laugh at their pleas and screams for help.

From this world of woe their souls depart
To the sea of flames where the punishment starts.
Despair and sorrow, for they're lost forever
Forgiveness for such on the twelfth of never.

And lo the Lord shall come in fire
Those who oppose him shall soon expire.
Pay heed to the words of our little Christina
Unite yourself with your Lord and Redeemer.

G F B

Peace

Peace at last! How nice it sounds
A feeling of freedom! Oh how it abounds
Rise up and be counted and help bring it about
Shout from the rooftops - we've just had enough.

The sixties have turned into the seventies
The eighties have made their way into the nineties
We shattered! After all those years
Violence has claimed the senseless death of many we held dear.

Sceptics have said the gulf is too wide
So let us build bridges to stem the tide
Listen politicians - you have the expertise
To take on board and help solve all those issues.

Tis great to see you come together
All very wise men! Who want to make it happen
Grasp those extended hands of friendship
Waste no time - your efforts have seen the candlelit.

Love and respect for all parties - is all we need.
Confidence in the future - let us sow the seed
Of one another culture - let us be tolerant!
Be seen to comfort one another ne'er more to confront!

Let us not care who shakes what hand
Or on whose cheek that caress will land
'To live and let live' is all we ask
So please carry on until you've finished the task.

B Caldwell

Drifting Into Winter

As I drift through the lanes,
To find tranquillity and peace.
With the beauty of the changing season,
Plants have respect to say the least!
Trees with their golden leaves,
Once shed helps fertilize the land,
While the Evergreens seem greener,
For it's their turn to have their stand!

Grasses gone to seed and dying back,
All ready to beat the winter storm.
While the ferns are turning brown,
So the landscape takes a different form!
With the last of the years fruits,
Such as blackberry bushes alike.
A chance for the animals to take a feast,
Before the winter takes its first bite!

Farmers have brought their harvest in,
Machinery covered ready for next year.
The sun has lost its strength now,
Shorter days, for night is nearly here!
Some birds sing out their chorus,
While other animals find homes to sleep.
But it's my turn to drift back now,
For a nice fire is my retreat!

Ann Beard

Clouds

I'm lying here in bed, watching the clouds race by.
Such fancies through my head, like clouds in the sky,
In fantastic shapes come. All sizes and shapes are they.
Some have the greatest fun frolicking in their play.

They are the happy ones, and scurry with laughing glee
O'er any path that comes, they are so glad to be free!
Of little white billows their dresses, of fleecy white
With goffered edges, like pillows, which are ironed just right

Then striding, with black face, at their happy, jolly game,
That just then was a race, an ugly grey shape came,
And with a loud harsh cry, ordered them out of his way,
Scared, they started to fly, much too frightened to stay.

But a thin agile cloud saw their sorrowful plight
And he, refusing to be cowed, decided to requite,
And coming to their aid, gave a shrill cry of rage
Made the bully so afraid, he looked quite grey with age

Then they passed along out of sight of mine eyes.
Soon comes a merry throng with bright shining faces
They pass too quickly on. For others soon take their places,
And on these the sun shone. So very dainty they were

With delicate pink edges. These not a breath did stir
For the winds gave their pledges to guard them all they could
For who would wish to harm these? They just went as they would
On such a gentle breeze. Then out came the Sun

With a broad happy smile and for him there were none
Who wouldn't linger awhile, but none of them guessed
Until it was too late he took them towards the West
And the end of their Fate!

D Ventris

31

Freedom

Oh joy, oh bliss a week alone
You and your son away from home.
No being wife or step-mother
Cook, cleaner, chauffeur of lover.
To soak in the bath my idea of heaven
To stay up late; well 'til after eleven.
Lay in bed until I'm ready to rise.
Eat what I want however unwise
Take the dog for long walks
On the 'phone having girlie talks.
Bryan Adams blaring away
Again and again through out the day.
No making drinks or washing up.
Just one plate and just one cup.
But come Thursday I am sure to say
I really wish you weren't away.

Cris Kingshott

Lovely Weather For Ducks

I can see great clouds forming,
They'll soon be filling the sky.
Where are my wellies and raincoat,
I aim to keep myself dry.

I'm thinking of going for a paddle,
Where the garden used to be.
There once was a sea of grass,
But now there's only a sea.

The weatherman says it will rain,
No matter how bad it looks.
Someone is bound to say,
'It's lovely weather for ducks.'

Rose Green

Heaven's Breath

Oh winter wind with ice cold chill,
Heaven's breath wailing so loud and shrill,
Ice Maiden's veil cloaking the ground,
Thy relentless roar the only sound.

From the north thou blowest with furious force,
No regard for life along thy course,
Proud trees bow to thy furore with broken limbs,
Thou hast total disrespect for all manner of things.

Thy vigour increases with frenzied blow,
Whipping and swirling the fresh lain snow,
In tumultuous sea, clouds race by,
Awaiting thy final death knell sigh.

Calm at last,
A breather thou takes,
Till next mighty onslaught,
From Heaven's Gate.

Janet Tinkler

A Psalm

I was meant to be - the word says so.
However I was conceived, in love, in lust, by mistake,
I was meant to be - the word says so.

My God saw me being formed, watched over the shaping, the
moulding;
Saw the human anger, the bitterness,
The lack of caring on my father's part.

But my Heavenly Father knows His purpose for me -
He knows it - has worked upon me, shaping, moulding, correcting,
leading -
He will do it - He will fulfil . . . but I wonder still
How much more moulding, shaping there is still to do.

(Based on Psalm 139)

Jean Hanford

If Tomorrow Never Came

If tomorrow never came for us
And today was the last day
We ever touched
I'd regret the things I've said and done
But most of all, the happiness to come

If we never spoke again
And I didn't have the chance
To let you know the way I feel
The way my heart beats faster
When you're near

Will you ever know just how much?
Will I ever speak the words?
My heart longs you to know
Just how much I care
And how I love you so

Will I ever make it right?
Will I ever realise that you
Are everything I want, and need
That life just wouldn't do

Don't let me hurt you now
Or ever
Don't let me hold you back
And never, let me make you feel
You aren't loved

There's no-one I can ask
Or tell
And no-one else who fills my heart
The way you do, I love you

Carolyn R Cunningham

Challenge

What was hidden behind her eyes?
The twinkle has gone and it makes to realise
That pain from the dark is still black
And more than she can handle now she is back,
In the world of no surprise.

Is her illness going to revive
The pattern of behaviour that reduced her size?
To that of an ice blade upon a track
What was hidden?

Suddenly without warning she eats supplies
Of goodies bought before her demise,
She's prepared no longer take the flack
For the bodily figure she does lack,
So she does again to the challenge rise
But what was hidden?

Carol Dunn

The Girl I Love

I wonder why I love you so
As you're not the only girl I know
There's one thing clear that when
            You are near
My heart goes pitter patter
Your hair is like the flowing breeze
And smile just like the sun
Oh how I wish that you would be mine
And make me the happiest one.

Roy Williams

Our Yvonne

I was sitting late one night
Thinking what's going on
The house, the job, you know
Then I thought of our Yvonne

I thought of her years ago
A mass of Golden Curls
And when I think of her again
She's still our little girl

It's difficult to show your love
To someone who's not here
Especially to someone
You really hold so dear

I'm trying to say we love you
I hope you understand
We hate you being so far away
In that far and distant land

We worry about that man Hussain
We think he's very mad
We worry about our daughter
Come home and make us glad

How do you say you love her
Without making such a scene
How do you say your wonderful
With words you really mean

How do you say your proud of her
I think your very strong
How do you say we love you
I get the words all wrong

I'm trying to say we love you
I'm trying to say well done
I'm trying to say your beautiful
Our lovely girl Yvonne

It's difficult by letter
It's not the same by phone
It's hard to say we care for you
It's easier when your home

We think about you all the time
I think you know we care
We pray that God looks after you
All the time your there

All our love Mum and Dad

Edward Williams Senior

In The Kitchen

A place for many cosy chats
Seems like mum was always there
And the back door leading to the garden
With roses scenting the air

And family would gather around
The table for a get together
Uncles aunts cousins and all
Or a cuppa when fed up with the weather

We always found a seat for them all
No matter how many came
The chairs came from all over the house
How I wish I could live it again

The family pulled together as one
Extra help given where it was needed
And the family honour was not to be tarnished
A thing that most families heeded

I don't like the earth as it is today
It's all so alien to me
If only I could walk in the old kitchen door
In the land that used to be

Adela Llewellyn

A Secret Cove

As I wonder on my travels
Exploring every corner on my way.
The excitement of what I find,
Reveals treasures hard to say!

Down a long steep twisting road,
Through the white sparkling cliffs
Capped with the growth cascading,
Just like a green snow drift.

For as the sea comes crashes in,
Then rebounds off the cliffs face.
Sends the water flying in the air,
Like diamonds floating in outer space!

Warm and cosy in this cove,
Tranquil time just drifts past.
For here was a place undisturbed,
Away from our hectic lives at last!

I've found the beauty of this world,
Which no man could ever buy.
God created all this for us,
So don't spoil it or pass it by!

Ann Beard

The Ending Of A Day

Sun setting closes the day
Daily chores kept at bay
While reflecting on the past day
Evening activities gave way
Bed time finally has its say
Peaceful thoughts sleepily sway.

Alan Jones

Paper Aerobatics

Lovers of the empire we aspire,
package product of neurosis network
where did we go   ?
We went through a computer window,
mother earth to digital mouse
temperate teenage kiss
my coca cola lips.

Urgent embrace to cyberspace
all systems down in star trek land,
privatisation forth Reich elite
another family is thrown on the street   !
Everyone's a film star
fellowship is a good thing
but empty words don't mean a thing.

Tripping beyond advert time
a bankers card for overdraft,
today a cat was given a new home
Gladys died due to lack of hospital beds.
Your child is fed
industrial strength bonded lead,
the mute nomad drives.

Mr President became a film star
Mr President became a rock star,
that technocrat is a mother of chat
so what do I say,
there's a new institution I went to yesterday
the solid state digital voice,
but I prefer my lover's kiss.

Jeremy Jones

44

Undervalued Values

Through suffering I've learned well
The rarity of love and joy
Taken too lightly by most, and squandered
As if leaves on a tree in autumn
But to us cursed few, in constant winter
The tearful icicles still cling
Until melted by warm affection
As the season does in spring

Come then kind people all,
With warmth and kindness be
That I might forget the past
Filled with pain and sorrow by me.

M Hutchings

Angel In The Street

I saw an angel
In the street today.
Fair of form, fair of face,
Angel wings hid,
'Midst snowy folds of lace.
The sun,
Shone,
Upon,
Its wondering eyes,
A tiny smile hovered,
Filled with joy.
Was it girl, or was it boy?
I only knew
The baby was an angel.
Filled with grace,
Sent with love,
From a heavenly place

Vivette

The - Circle - Of - Love?

Love - is - like - a - circle - going - round -
And - round - in - the - time?
We - all - hope - that - while - here - on -
Earth - we'll - find - true - love - sublime?
It's - just - like - nothing - else - truly -
Plus - makes - us - feel - alive?
As - the - thrill - of - love - is - awesome -
And - helps - us - to - survive?
All - emotions - our - senses - and - every -
Touch - too?
Can - simply - seem - magic - when - two -
People - love - true?
Caring - plus - sharing - communication -
All - through?
A - life - where - pure - joy - will remain -
With - you - see?
Due - to - both - working - hard - for - the -
Circle - and - be?
Always - trying - their - best - to - keep -
That - circle - going - round?
Because - if - one - neglects - this - then -
It'll - roll - to - the - ground?
So - love - equally - and - don't - let -
Love - die? Be - true - to each - other -
Then - laugh - but - never - cry?

Margaret Alexander

Wallflowers In England

Virgilian velvet
lies within
these flowers

Imperial red and Dido's gold
maroon the deaths of kings
with lavender for rue
the faded rose of columbine
and chestnuts glossy brown
the yellow of the sun
all drowsing in their honeyed haze

And after boring years
of Caesar's Gaelic Wars
on May the third began
the glorious *Aeneid*

The window was ajar
and from the flowered wall
rolled wave on fragrant wave
which Virgil adumbrated
until the velvet scent became
transmuted into Latin

* It is believed that their seeds four petalled fragrant of many colours
were in the stone the Normans brought to England in 1066
(Botanical
Gardens, Cambridge)

Audrey Wilson

Jaffa Gate

The native bus climbed
　　The steep hills winding road
To its journey end
　　And a memory unforgettable

The sky was a glory
　　Of purple and gold
Set against this
　　In dark silhouette
The Jaffa Gate of old Jerusalem
　　Timeless forbidding and bold

I had made the trip
　　To the dead sea
The air was insufferably hot
　　Laced inevitably with the aroma of pot

There were live chickens on board
　　And a frustrated goat
With no room to butt
　　Or fresh air to bleat
But that glory on return
　　Made the pilgrimage complete

　　Bryn Bartlett

Forever Near

For those of you who have
lost someone,
to God's eternal sleep,
take comfort in the knowing,
their presence is yours to keep.

They may not be in sight to
you,
yet they never leave your mind,
you sense them, and you feel them
yet you dismiss your precious find.

The air we breathe is out of sight,
yet we accept it gladly,
yet when our loved ones lose
their shell,
we really feel it badly.

Next time you feel their gentle breeze,
or their touch so very tender,
a familiar fragrance may fill the air
remember they are the sender.

They love you now, as they did then
and love bonds never break,
their spirit which is their true self,
is free and ever awake.

Next time you feel your loved one
drawing close,
or whispering in your ear,
remember your memories one by one,
and they will prove their near.

A Frame

A True Story
War Time Experience Of A District Nurse

One very dark and dreary night,
There were no stars, and no moonlight
I had a baby to deliver
In a gypsy camp, down by the river.

The journey started on my bike
The rest of the way I had to hike
Across some fields I had to go
It was very difficult. This I know

But alas and then alack
Somehow I wandered from the track
This was a predicament, nothing to match
I found myself in a cabbage patch

In my troubles, I saw a spark
An ember shining through the dark.
I hurried forward and found a gate,
Hoping I was not too late.

By the faint glimmer of my lamp
I knew I had found the gypsy camp.
The babe was born in the early morn
So I travelled home in the light of dawn.

Olive Brailee

Whatever

Whatever, is it coming too,
Each and every day,
The things, you hear.
And, what you see,
You hope, don't come your way.

You see neglect with children!
And with animals too,
You, also hear of 'murders',
And a rape or two.

Sometimes there are 'muggings'
And breaking 'in to stores'
And then again, there's breakings
If we forget, to 'lock our doors'

Of all these, 'things that happen'
We have to 'make a test'
And tell our 'local station'
And hope they'll 'do their best'.

E B Holcombe

52

Loving Me Loving You
(Dedicated to Stephen forever my love)

Be mine forever stay in my arms
kiss me tenderly, deliver all your charms.

Make me shiver with excitement
that's what it's all about,
keep that flame burning,
and never let it go out.

I'm yours, you are mine
I want to be with you all the time.

To lie next to you every night
to hold your body so very tight.

Wanting you in more ways than one
for my pleasure and for fun.

Making love with you is wonderful and true,
living without you, I'd be forever blue.

Julie Ann

Summer Delights

The summer breezes whisper in my ear.
Telling of warm days and scented air,
of languorous eves when love is known
Waking to the chorus of birds at dawn.

Walking out on the sun-drenched beaches
Fishes darting in the clear blue sea,
Seagulls screeching on their darting flight
And colours enhanced in the summer light.

Sitting in the garden at the close of day.
Bees flying home on their honeyed way.
Colours and scents of the vibrant flowers.
Bringing delight to our summer bowers.

Strolling through fields of waving corn
Where poppies their scarlet cloaks are worn.
The perfume of blossom on hedgerows around
And winged insects like jewels abound.

Homeward we tread our senses alight
To the beauty of nature, the blessing of light,
Our hearts on fire with all we have seen,
Of the countryside and all that it means.

Emma Hunt

Pillow Talk

Oh! with what sweet surrender, when each day's
                          a tough back bender,
We at night commit tired bodies to our beds!
Having soaked in bubble baths, after weeding garden paths,
Time at last to 'count those sheep, rest weary heads.

When with your spouse you're tucked up tight,
                          have bid each other fond goodnight
Then turning over, snuggle down on favourite side,
When nearly, so it seems, you are in the land of dreams
Your husband snorts, a snore reports, mouth gaping wide!

Sleepily around you inch, and with your fingers bottom pinch,
Which doesn't meet, upon receipt, with his approval!
He then declares it wasn't him who was creating such a din,
So you threaten to uproot - make a removal!

Deciding both to try again, this time from snoring to refrain,
Upon your pillows you again drift into sleep.
Until, much louder than before, and with a snore more like a roar,
Your sure its lions hunting prey - about to leap!

With frustration and despair, you rise resigned and leave him there,
Finding peace on the lounge sofa, curl up tight,
When the night gives way to dawn, stretching
                          cramped limbs you widely yawn
His greeting clear, 'Good morning dear, sleep well last night?'

Marcia Elizabeth Jenkin

55

Autumn's Garland

Autumn has dressed her mannequins
Memorably this time; I hold
A golden sequin in the prudence
Of my palm, unite several others
In colours I can not compliment with words.

I placed the garland around
Your inventive fairy forehead;
Maternal flashbulbs beamed
Imprints onto my serotonin screen.

In my years to match this season
I will again watch your fledgling form,
Airbrushing the dank walls
In the unrivalled kaleidoscope
This years autumn has hypnotised for me.

Michele Glazer

Di

Her spirit of dancing flowers
Her movements such pure joy
Within her daily worth
Oh where is she now

Her smiling face
Most beautiful of eyes
Her joy such of laughter
When she's with wonderful boys

Within this brain
I see her every and where
In long flowing gowns
A woman of every man's dream

If in this world
Of what we seek and do
Why this dove
Should fly all unto you

You've taken her soul
Long before she's old
What of all our dreams
Pity is not we greed

Her flowing charms
Babies in arms
When all are sick
Paper's so very quick
As on every page
Such beauty behold
Lost forever
Our dancing princess

E T Ward

The Evacuee

It was like wearing white at a funeral
That's how I felt,
It was like being the odd one out
That's what I remember,
Part of me wanted to go home
Part of me wanted to scream
That's all I remember,
Maybe that's all I want to remember.

Sophie Laskowski

Not Recently

Not recently, nor after careful thought,
        but on an impulse, in day's early pride,
        wheeling my bicycle (too awed to ride)
        spring bright on every side
I entered Hampton Court.

Not recently; sad years between so bleak
        with war and waste and godlessness and greed.
        But memory that, steadfast, does not heed
        matters that interplead,
holds that prized morning vivid and unique.

Three score of years have gone upon their way
        since that May garden, dew-jewelled, washed with rain,
        those palace courts. I have gone there again
        seeking, always in vain,
the unsought magic of the magic day.

It's not some morning's outing that has grown
        in memory, to play so prime a part,
        perpetual partner of a wondering heart,
        wondering at the art
that made me, passing there, made me alone

(none else was there) a witness of the vast
        pageant of prelates, princes, queens and kings,
        statesmen, advisors on world-warping things,
        scholars whose ponderings
gave Holy Writ an English voice at last.

For I that morning was appointed one
       with those, fleet-footed in their eager haste
       or - less impetuous - who calmly paced
       the path I traced;
upon those myriad missions long since done.

Martin Summers

Trying To Deal With Sudden Death

Why did you leave me alone my love?
Alone and afraid of the dark.
You know when you left,
you left me behind, to live with a broken heart.

Why did you leave me alone my love,
why did you leave so soon?
If I wasn't afraid of what people would say,
I'd sit and bay at the moon.

How could you leave me so heart sore?
Grief and anger reign,
there are no words that friends can say
that eases this awful pain.

Will the passing of time heal this hurt?
Time alone will tell,
wherever you are help me
now, live through this private hell.

Isabel McEwing

Life

It is a pleasurable experience
And it only happens once.
To some you are clever,
To others you're a dunce.
Maybe it is oxygen,
Maybe it is not,
But whatever causes intellect
You live with what you've got!
It is how you use it
That causes men to say.
He is an upright fellow,
You can trust him all the way.

D R Thomas

A Vegetarian Dream

It's prostrate trouble I have got.
So many men have it too
Doctor says two ways to treat, so what?
One is surgery other a pill
Father had surgery it proved to be 'kill'
At 76 still useful to all
He fell victim to doctor's skill
So what other ways are now on call?
If mother nature's with us still
She must have something for us all
'Stands to reason' says my brother
Reason has it then - no other.
Back to diet, it's no bother.
'Eat your greens up' says my mother
So it's 'vegy' this and 'vegy' that
And stop existence on 'snicks' and 'snacks'
But research still must have a say
It's what we pay for every day
So one small pill with doctor's blessing
And spuds and tomatoes and salad with dressing.
And tomorrow we hope and for which we pray
A body so fit we'll be here and we'll stay.

F J Simpson

Perfect Days

Do you remember those days
When we laughed together
I could feel your heart beat
It was as soft as a feather.

I run my fingers through your hair
In silky strands it lay
I buried my head deep in your heart
United we'll find a way.

I gave you all I could
Helping you fill your tum
It made you very happy
You had become a first class mum.

We named her little Becky
We looked her in the eyes
We told her that we loved her
She let out a great big cry.

Soon she left to find her dream
Without her it wasn't home
So we went on a package trip
Old, no teeth and a tour of Rome.

Life is nearly at an end
Let's take it all the way
Every time we take a breath
It could be the last day.

There is no more tomorrow
Today we've seen the last
All we can do now
Is look back at our past.

Philip Meikle

Recriminations

I can't forget the unkempt tramp
I passed the other day.
He only asked for something small
To take his pain away.
With withering scowl and bitter words
I sent him on his way.
It certainly wasn't my business
To ease his pain away.

And then I got to wondering
Why I had acted so.
If that had been my Saviour
Would I have scorned Him so?
Without a kind and helpful word
Would I have let Him go?
Would I have turned my back on Him,
As I did on derelict Joe?

Christ always loved the outcasts,
The misfits, the forlorn,
The rejects classed as useless.
That's why our Lord was born.
The image of my Saviour,
The Herald of the Dawn,
Gazed sadly through this stranger
Whom I had dared to scorn.

Sadly I pondered my actions;
Forlornly thought of the past;
Wondered could I have done better;
Regretted lost chances. Aghast
At my ruthless behaviour
In scorning the weak and downcast.
Forgive me, compassionate Saviour,
For I am the real outcast.

Monica O'Sullivan

Funny Isn't it? Or Is It?

A rubber-band is on the floor -
Must pick it up, (not be a bore!)
With my two sticks, I shift and shove . . .
. . . to hook it safe, but will it move?
I try and try, the whole 'world' watching:
'What's she doing?' I hear them asking.
I hear me saying: 'I strive in vain!'
But look! What's this? I try again . . .
. . . I've caught it up! (didn't need a brain).
Just persevere, and don't despair;
But hold it up, and tell them all!
Or - would you rather risk a fall?

Ada Betty Harrison

Number One Poultry

I waited obediently at the crossing
    Where the red man bade me stay
And stood just idly gazing
    At the building over the way

A blue plaque caught my attention
    Affixed to the elaborate facade
Once on that site it made mention
    Lived Thomas Hood when a lad

I recalled his nostalgic phrases
    In his 'I remember' lines
And how he lauded in golden verses
    His early life and times.

But surely that house was a cottage
    Far away from this busy street
Where robins built and bees could forage
    Amongst the lilac blossoms sweet

The plaque my illusions had shattered
    A bus pulled up with a screech
The green man my day-dreaming scattered
    The other side now I could reach.

I stopped where Griffin scanned
    The site on which a home once stood
The Listening Bank's head office spanned
    The birthplace of Thomas Hood

Inside, many workers spent their day
    Scrutinising computer screens
Above the ground where Tom would play
    Acting out his boyhood dreams

Does his youthful spirit live on yet
    Technology inspiring his poetry
And would he write a 'Song of the Internet'
    Dedicated to Number One Poultry?

June Mary Harris

Wedding

Sands of Mombasa
Do you still remember me?
As for me,
Just a memory is not enough.
Therefore,
A tiny part of you,
I have captivated in a jar.
When I look at you
My imagination
Breaks the barriers of this alien land
And magnifies the contents
Of this jar.
As far and wide and real as you.
I feel the soothing caress
Of your million pebbles
On my grown up soles again.
Do you know my best days,
The picnic days of life,
I imprinted on your vastness.
Or has the Indian Ocean
Washed away my little girlish footprints
Forever from your face.
Often when I am lonely,
Which is more often than not,
And lie quietly in my bed at night,
I always think of you;
Stretched over
Miles and miles of lovely beaches
My eyes spill out an ocean,
Which like restless waves
Runs forwards
To kiss your fatherly face
Again and again in fancy.

And when the tide of tears recedes
I go to sleep solaced;
Thinking that I have taken
Some particles of you
Into my bottomless depths.
Sometimes,
When all my tears are not enough
I think of going back
Once again to you.
To lie in your lap
But very deep;
Embedded beyond the reaches
Of the Indian Ocean.
To remain wedded to you
In a fossilised form
For a millennium at least to come.

Sophia Ahmed

The Child (And Father) Consider Love

The child sits and ponders.
The chair upon which it sits ceases creaking,
Silent in reverence of the young searching soul.
What is love?

The man with vacant detachment ponders.
The most sensuous of all enigmas
Elation, pain, joy, sorrow all tied.
What is love?

The child sits patiently.
The man regards the child.
Where does he start
What is love?

An answer forms but evaporates.
As elusive as the thistle seed
Tossed on a summer's breeze.
What is love?

The man looks about him for an answer.
The woman catches his glance and smiles
The answer reveals itself with cool refreshment.
What is love?

My son
My daughter
The lady by my side
What is love?
Angel

Philip Knight

For Diana

Dreaming, dreaming, ever dreaming
   Diana of you,
O our Heart, cease beating, beating,
   Love's deep sorrows through,
Till our sleeping Brain is victim
   Of its deepest grief,
All the night our lost love seeking,
   Finding no relief.

Cease, our Heart! O cease your throbbing,
   Who can bear such pain?
Cease, our Voice! For who such sobbing
   Longer can sustain?
Yet our Eyes flow, weeping, weeping,
   Bitter tears we shed,
Voices whisper in our sleeping,
   Diana is dead.

O the cruel, cruel dagger
   Plunging in our breast,
Prostrate in our fever tossing
   Out of reason pressed,
O we loved you, loved you, loved you,
   Search for you we must,
Stay Death's ruthless hand, dissolving
   Loveliness to dust.

Were there ever eyes more tender?
   Voice more soft or sweet?
Ministers more kind and gentle
   Than your hands and feet?
Here is all-consuming anguish,
   Loving's price is paid,
All our life, our light, our longing,
   In your grave are laid.

Flowers we bring to heap upon you,
  Blossoms fading fast,
Autumn's leaves descend around you,
  Summer overpast,
 Winter's snow will soon be falling,
  Stark the haze will stand,
Ice will freeze our Heart from bleeding,
  Quench the burning brand.

William Mead

Reconciliation

Hush, don't cry, let me hold you once more;
   Oh Lord, how I longed for this to be.
On losing you to that man of straw,
   I replaced you with cold misery.

Rest safe in my arms, my bonny lass,
   Still as fair as in your bridal year.
A beauty, angels cannot surpass,
   Nor the sculptor 'Time' make disappear.

God made you mine, with his grace bestowed,
   But yet, there was the devil to pay.
His due was our parting, which I owed
   To a rake's tongue in silver array.

I wept bitter tears, pricking as thorns,
   Tart drops of the ache flooding my heart.
I cried the dark nights through to their dawns,
   In mourning the lonely cuckold's part.

His honeyed vows - he soured them all,
   He reneged and slunk for cover,
His shabby honour beyond recall,
   As he played the transient lover.

Your heart and my heart - two hearts broken,
   Sweetheart, let me pay you court again.
Nestle close, give me love's sweet token,
   Which is but a kiss, and end the pain.

Ron Dodd

Helpless Handicap

It seems so wrong to be whole
When another is fallen apart,
Yet what is there for me to do
To change the situation?
If I had the power to turn
Our places round, I do not
Believe I would find the courage
Or selflessness to do so.
Although I feel great pity
For one such as you, and want
To help you to a better life,
I have a small tolerance
Of your odd movements and disfigured speech.
I know this is wrong,
I hate to think in such a way,
But I do.
However my admiration for you
Overrides my fault -
I will help you.

Beverley Ann Haworth

A Magic Moment?

Another outing on a warm sunny day.
What can we do, where can we play?
The children at last find something to do.
So I take a stroll in pastures new.
The lane leads into a shady nook.
A scene meets my eyes from a picture book.
Red squirrels are softly playing
I focus my camera before they start straying.
But my noise makes them scamper away.
Anxious to make the most of the day.
I fetch my family so they can see.
The squirrels playing around the tree.
Eagerly I show them the little nook.
Expecting to see the squirrels afoot.
But they have all vanished, where can they be?
Honest! I really saw them, believe me.

Phyllis Dartnell

Inner Beauty

I imagine this world around me
And what it would be to see
They tell me trees are all sorts of green
I imagine what green could be

I picture a beautiful flower
From its touch and its smell
Though I cannot see it
It is beautiful, I can tell

I hear the summer birds singing
I hear a stream rushing by
I hear distant church bells ringing
I hear the world pass me by

I sense when there is danger
I know when it is calm
To feel the touch of a stranger
Who leads me by my arm

To go through life imagining
All sorts of wonderful things
Though I can't see with any vision
I see all the beauty from within.

Sandra Quigley

Lost Love

Thirty-six years ago!
Why does it haunt me so,
That long-lost love-affair?
That chance meeting on the train
From Manchester to Euston;
The instant greeting in our eyes
And recognition in our souls,
Never experienced before or since.

Three months passed; it had to end.
It could not last; we could not mend
That broken dream, for it would seem
Such love was not for mortals meant,
But came to us by accident . . .

Where is she now,
My enchanting companion?
The angel who suddenly entered my life,
And as suddenly left it -
And left me bewildered;
Is she another man's much-cherished wife?

Edward Francis

Hearts Of Love

I love your smile
The style of your hair.
I love your perfume
The clothes that you wear.
Your my little miss perfect
Gentle as a dove.
Your the girl in my dreams
The one, that I love.

You return what I give
And never just take.
Our loves like the melody
That drifts over the lake.
It's the song angels sing
As their instruments play.
To the sound our hearts beating
They dance, everyday.

A love born in heaven
Of this I am sure.
Where else in this world
Could love flow so pure.
Our two hearts entwined
Together for life.
Vowed love for eternity
As Husband, and Wife.

Dennis N Davies

Triumph-Ant

Deep in the Heart of the Forest lived a Colony of Ants you see?
A Colony of Ants whose Home was Beneath a Tree,
Their Daily existence from Dawn until Dusk
Was Much Akin to us, and that's Work to earn a Crust?

One Special Ant called David it seems?
Was entrusted with leadership and divided his friends into Teams,
Although very small they were very strong indeed
And apart from their agility they were gifted with Speed,

Until one day an Ant Eater arrived
And by the time it had finished not many survived,
Nicknamed Goliath because of its Build
The Ant Eater ate everything that it killed.

David decided to use his Brain and his strength
To dig a large Hole of Considerable Length,
After covering the Hole he decided to hide
And await the outcome as the Ant Eater fell inside?

The Moral of this Story is Big or Small?
We can all end up with a Considerable fall,
David our Hero to others it was acclaimed
Has his name clearly Written in the Ants Hall of Fame.

The Bible it seems tells of another David's Name?
One who also gained considerable Fame,
Many Years ago in a time gone by
In a Time when a Stone hit Goliath between the Eye?

Triumph-Ant to the end?

Robert James Bridge

80

Autumn

The joy of autumn
Sprinting out the door
Tumbling, rolling and laughing
In red, golden brown leaves
The time to be silly has come
Free from summer
The glory of autumn
The excitement
No one knows how I feel
No one on earth except me
Bare trees, branches stretching out
Into the beautiful sky
What glory of autumn
More and more leaves falling on top of my head
I must be the only child in the world
I'm so happy
A big garden with so many trees
So many colours
I could make a mountain
Out of the leaves
I love autumn
The carpet of leaves is waiting for me
Just me and only me!
No one can stop me from
Fun, fun, fun
Birds going away
Its goodbye birds
A perfect garden
It's very dark
The joy of autumn

Ryrie Oag

October Days

Smells of gardens, dank and wet,
Compost heaps as black as jet.
With pungent smells as bonfires blaze,
October brings her golden days.

Time to clear the flower beds,
Gone to seed, tall Poppy heads.
Musty decomposing leaves,
Where the lazy Spider weaves.

Chrysanthemums are still in bloom,
Their floppy, moppy heads assume
Their cycle very near complete,
Release aromas, bittersweet.

With scents of black earth, freshly dug,
A cheeky Robin - fat and smug,
Seeks unsuspecting worms and flies,
With ever watchful beady eyes.

As patiently he'll watch me toil,
Dislodging insects from the soil.
Then perching on my idle spade,
Was king of all that he surveyed.

Mid scarlet berries vivid flush,
And old Crab Apple's rosy blush,
Virginia creeper hugs the wall,
With blazing colours of the fall.

Misty gardens, dripping wet,
Compost piled behind wire net,
Dying bonfires, smoky haze,
How I love October days.

Hilda Jones

Alone In The Night

I awake of the owl twitting the night away
The full moon arises
The stars are glancing over us
All around us, the sound of musical people
I'm sleep in silence, without any love for me
I feel lonely and quite ashamed of my love
For someone, but whom
I cried my heart out of desperate at night
Why I'm not like any girl
Who likes to drink and do anything for the boy
I feel empty inside,
I see the summer clouds going across your face
That you praise your world
We listen to another song,
As we made love, all night long
Whatever will be I will always forever remember the good times

Nina Short

Love

Life is good, until the passion goes
And go it must, for we are but mortal men
Living out, out three score years and ten
Some may achieve greatness
Others fall by the wayside
Like a grain of wheat, rotting forever,
On the wings of time
For time, is the only certain thing
We are born, we live, we die, and then
What matters, if we are great or small
Or rich or poor, or fairest men
Always take love, when you find it
If you find it, hold it fast
Do not drain it or profane it.
Nurture it, and make it last

R Swarbrick

Where Are They Now?

Where are they now?
Those precious hours I miss,
Those stolen hours of bliss
We snatched along the way.
When we would hug and kiss
And wallow in love's play.

Where are they now?
Those wings we had to fly
The freedom of the sky,
Those castles in the air.
Those hopes we held so high
Those dreams we loved to share.

Where are they now?
The words I loved to hear
You whisper in my ear.
Those eyes that brightly shone
So full of love sincere.
That now are sadly gone.

Where are they now?
The laughter and the tears
Cascading down the years.
The joy, anguish and pain.
The guilt and jealous fears
We suffered all in vain.

Where are they now?
Lost to the world maybe
But never so to me.
They always will remain
Fresh in my memory
Until we meet again.

J D Winchester

Creation And Destruction

On a lake shines golden sunlight.
Where a Lily blossoms white,
So pure, untouched, sacred.
Its petals flutter so gently,
Like butterflies in their flight,
Mysteriously inviting,
But so dangerous to touch.
The flower breaths so gently,
But its sighs can be heard for miles,
Screams of agony.
Persecution and torment fills the air,
Amongst the screams there is singing,
So sweet, so gentle,
But some how never heard.
Within the cloying, luscious flower,
There is bitterness, dispise and animosity,
That pulls you close with its elegance,
And as you touch it bites.
So hard the pain is eternal,
Although at first you don't feel the pain,
It grows with every day.
Soon the lily is weak.
Its petals now black,
Like the black that surrounds us.
Wilted through exhaustion,
Powerless and pathetic,
Holding only mere spasms of life.
Soon it will be the end.
Not only for the flower,
But for mankind.

J Lewis

My Darling

You looked at me with eyes so bleak
They said the words lips could not speak
Nine months said the doctors all they could give
I'll never forget that as long as I live
We loved each other, you and I
And now they say you are to die
How can I live without you how can I let you go
To another world beyond the stars a world I do not know
I only know that God lives there and
Will welcome you in arms that care
One day the call will come for me
To join you in eternity
I look forward to the time
When once more you will be mine
We'll sail once more on the ship of life
With all its problems joy and strife
Good things, bad things come our way
But still we find the time to pray
Until one more again we reach
The safety shore of God's own beach.

Sophie Godfrey

Christchurch Meadow In Spring

Pink paduan cherry blossom framed heaven in a pure morning sky
Whilst the filled, vernal, Cherwell just wandered slowly by and why
Proud hazel with fresh green buds so finely wrought and well
> displayed
Stood smiling at the searching squirrel for its fall fallen nuts mislaid
Amidst the winter litter now thawed by springs' sure warm
> caressing
For which the seasons song birds in thanks gave an addressing
> blessing
Whilst watching the symbol of Bohun and crest and emblem of
> Lorraine
In form of penn sail, so serenely queenly, over flooded meadowland
> terrain
When then in imprecise 'zeitgeist' did suddenly boom out the bells of
> grand 'Old Tom'
Joined joyously in anthem by springs singing of an allelvia and an
> ending 'Te Deum'

D G Viall

Summer

We awaken from a meal of sleep refreshed with dreams,
Every sense on tiptoe; hearing the undersong of streams
Quicksilvering through the fields where it is now for ever;
Seeing the high hills standing with their knees in mist.

Gladly we arise to taste the hours of the ascending day,
To feel at home in happiness where everything is coming home
And nature is the spirit rendered visible.

Sunlight softly blazes from the chandelier of noon
Upon the lucid meadows flowering with delight
Beneath a canopy of butterflies. Trees shake out their shadows
In a green and flickering tracery, are budded with a breeze of birds.

Glimmering twilight fades into the amethyst of evening.
The stars appear like legends of a world of light
To shine through all their glittering hours while we're asleep.

Now that we are free from care, who would want another birth?
Days like this were all too rare - during our life on Earth.

Robert Gordon

To Be Ashamed

To never think of others
To never give a damn
To hide away in corners
To be ashamed
To be a man
To take all of the forest
To bring it to its knees
To pollute all of the rivers
To pollute all of the seas
To destroy the ozone layer
To poison all the air
To never think of others
To never really care

Alan Green

The Whistler

If you ever hear the Whistler,
Standing by the old Wish Well,
You should fear to be a listener
For he'll cast on you his spell.
And the willows and the birches
That are planted all around
Will not heed your cries of anguish
As you fall upon the ground.

But when time begins to darken
And the sun outlives the moon;
When the angels start to harken
Then the world is at its noon.
Will this sorrow never cease?
Does the story end with you?
Will he come at last to peace?
Does the Whistler's song end too?

Flittering shadows dance around him
And all creatures stop to hear
What the Whistler has to tell them:
Mortal anger, mortal fear.
So much hubris, so much gall,
Must we always show our might?
And we think we know it all
But the Whistler's always right!

Merlin Hanbury-Tenison (12)

91

Sunset Over The New Forest

T'was a lovely summers evening
    as we travelled those lonely roads
Our driver he was cautious
    and he knew the way to go
He was anxious for the ponies
    who roamed across the road
Or suddenly appeared as light was fading fast
Then in the distant sky we saw
    a sight that filled us all with 'awe'
The most wonderful sunset plain to see
    as if a promise of Eternity
For even though its rays we cannot always see
    the memory of that sunset still remains with me
But then you see - we were happy
    and in good company
So perhaps the title of this poem should be
    'The end of a perfect day - for me

Louis R Early

Believe

In my dream there's an angel I can see
In my dream there's an angel just for me
Now I wonder if the good Lord has picked me
To tell His lost souls what I see
Or is it something I just can't understand
Why my dreams help me see the Promised Land
Or maybe I just don't believe
That the good Lord walked this earth before me
To tell the truth I'm not sure what I see
All I know it was real to me
Now I hope I'll dream for ever more
To see some things I have seen before
Now my life has more meaning than before
I feel for certain we live for ever more.

Thomas Boyle

The Joy Of Poetry

The sun is shining brightly, the month is May,
I have just finished reading, 'Day by Day'.
The poems there written, give so much pleasure,
To Authors and Readers, so much to treasure.
One poem, I relate to as an insider,
Identically like me, entitled 'The Spider'.
Words expressed bring joys, also tears,
Memories of sad happenings, and some happy years.
Feelings and words, that pull at heartstrings,
Immense joy that sharing with others, Poetry brings.
Never assuming, to become one of the greats,
Many poems therein, to my life relates.
Hope nobody will mind, if more words I'll write,
That will paint a picture so, Poetically bright.

June F Allum

There Will Be No Laughter On The Streets

There will be no laughter, on
the streets, where found
you, in all your glory. Where
the patriots dwell beneath
the silence, that is my home
beneath the silence, I dwell
upon.

There will be no laughter on
the streets, where we
wandered oft astray only
to find, in the absence
of day a new world, in
the darkness.

There will be no laughter on
the streets, as I heard
you call my name, we have
come and gone, we have
loved forever and soon
the morning, will take
you away.

Robert Robb

Winter Solstice

Through England's bleak mid-winter
The cold, the frost and snow
The void was filled with fairy lights
The darkness was aglow
They wallowed in wild parties
They swallowed up large beer
Bedecked the trees with tinsel
Jolly Santa's drove reindeer
For Jesus was a legend
And Father Christmas real
They all conceived a fable
With a backdrop surreal
Stonehenge still stood; the answer
For tangible it seems
But stones alone yield coldness
An idol Druid's dream.

In England's bleak mid-winter
The people groaned and moaned
Were searching for reality
Yet searching for a stone
The truth is set before them
The way is clear and bright
So . . . why are they still groping
And searching for that light
The truth has always been there
'Midst mistletoe and holly
And Jesus gives eternal life
Not Santa Claus' so jolly

The key has been provided
No mere ephemeral stone
Or other transient objects
To worship as a throne
The door to Heaven's open
Symbolic as the star
Which led wise men to Jesus
And shepherds from afar
At last there was an answer
To mans incessant sin
The door is standing open
And peace is found within
The saddest song is Solstice
The pagan's heartfelt cry
Rejection of the way and truth
But they were sold a lie.

Judy Studd

February Phenomenon

February brings the rain thaws the frozen lake again.
February '98 is a memorable date - why?
I'll tell you - its surprise was noted by
Barometer rise
Of temperatures above the 'norm'
To beat the warmth of Benidorm,
Awakening the primrose sweet,
Scattering daisies at our feet
While crocuses, their cups of gold
Or pied in purple stripes - unfold.
E'ere Valentine - the mating time
Had dawned - the birds in song sublime
Were chasing, courting this year's spouse
And building nests their eggs to 'house'.
Let us beware - the March winds shrill
(That stir the dancing daffodil)
Might oust the warm - wet gulf-stream flow
And cool the land with falls of snow.
So, shed no 'clout' 'cos its for sure
A winter back' lash we'll endure.

Frances Cox

Scraddlyboo

I say, is it true
that the Scraddlyboo
has a lump
on the end of his nose,
I need hardly mention
how such a dimension
would add
to that poor creature's woes.

For the Illiaghbad,
who's a bit of a cad
and at parties
is much in demand,
told his cousin, the Phrew,
that the Scraddlyboo
was going,
quite rapidly, mad.

He had taken to bed,
so the Illiagh said,
without even washing
his feet,
and, as everyone knows,
a Scaddlyboo's toes
are never
considered discreet.

Then the Phrew, who was wise,
but who wore a disguise
for his head
was exceedingly small,
took to walking the land
with his shoes in his hand,
in the hope
he would grow very tall.

The effect that this had
on the Illiaghbad,
who was cousin,
remember, to Phrew;
was to make him despair,
pullout half his hair
and take himself
off to the zoo.

Robert Lindsay

No Need To Shiver

No need to shiver
Come
Let me wrap you up
In a bunch of marigolds
Can you feel their warmth?
See how the lark watches
With
Envious eyes
He can only enjoy
The warmth
Of
The sun.

Jan Duncan

Love

What is there in life if there is no love?
This gift that comes, from God above.
It's in our hearts and in our mind.
If only this love, we could find.
We need to feel, that someone's there,
To share our troubles and our cares.
We need to share, a warm embrace.
And see the love in someone's face.
We need a partner who understands,
Who will walk through life with us,
                    hand in hand.
Yes we need a partner, but also
                    a friend.
Who will walk by your side,
                    till the journey's end.

Eileen Cambruzzi

My Endless Nightmare

School was a living hell,
I tread the halls in fear of the monster that haunted me.
A minute seemed like hours as I awaited the torture.
Each day was a continuous nightmare,
The vision of his face eternally tormented my childhood.
My flesh creeped at the mention of his name,
My blood ran cold from his glaring blood shot eyes,
And towering figure that hung over me.
My confidence was shattered by his harrowing words,
Each one struck like a dagger digging deep into my soul.
Free time was once a pleasure but now an endless terror.
He persecuted my life leaving me feeling worthless.
Sweet smiles and cheery chatter covered the emptiness I now felt.
Not once was I free not even at home,
His terrorising of the day lay with me at night.
My tears could overflow any riverbank.
How can I be free from him persecuting me?

Lisa McGuinness

The Forest Of Barrowdene

To stroll through the forest on a warm summers day.
Away from the crowds, the noise and the fray.
To walk beneath the towering trees,
And feel on my face the light summer breeze.
As the warmth of the sun caresses my skin,
Peace and contentment I feel within.

The birds are singing in the branches above,
The lark, the linnet, the sparrow, the dove.
Each one sings in a hearty voice, a song of love and sweet rejoice.
Whilst the babbling brook that flows below,
O'er stones on which the green moss grows,
Wends its way through the forest green
To join the river at Barrowdene.

As I cross the babbling brook. Upon the bridge I pause and look
Around me at the glorious trees,
That gently sway in the light summer breeze.
The oak, the elm and the maple tree
Created by nature for all to see,
And beneath the trees in green all around
Foxglove, Willow Herb, Primrose and Poppy,
All growing wild beneath the green canopy.

Squirrels are playing high in a tree,
Occasionally pausing to look down at me.
A stranger who stands and watches them play
As they chase each other up and away
Higher into the branches above
To join the lark, the linnet, the dove,
And there to remain high above ground
To appear once again when no one's around.

As I leave the babbling brook behind
And up the wooded hill I climb.
The forest creatures with watchful eye,
Lie silent and hidden as I pass them by,
Until at last from the shade of the trees
I step into the sunlight and the warm summer breeze.
I sense the earth power in the land,
Its health and richness I understand.
With green grass below and blue skies above,
I feel at one with the land that I love.

Joseph Michaels

Out Of Touch

On a balcony in the sky to plane's sound
Years have passed by since his slippers touched the ground.
He has a scar right from his head down to his toes.
He said 'this height doesn't stop me being so low'
Some social lady brings him food weekly.
Someone said, she said 'He's as crazy as can be'.
On the thirtieth floor for the thirtieth year
In his bathroom there's a well where he drowns his broken
tears.
There was a Mrs a long long time ago
But you know how stories and gossip flow.
Apparently he adored her, loved her too much!
So she left him thirty floors up out of touch.

Ritchie Farrell

Invisible Grieve

(Dedicated to my Grandfather John Bowie
With a soul to take a bond to break)

I feel your presence surrounding me
Your invisible face I long to see
How my arms ache to hold you now
I lie to my heart we'll see you somehow.

No-one can see the tears that I cry
The pain I feel at not saying good-bye
I try to pretend soon it will ease
I place my hand on my heart begging help,
Us please.

Your strength opens my eyes to every hard new day
Your warmth I feel inside when my heart gives way
Your pride makes me smile hoping you are too
But it's your love that gives me the reason I need
To live without you.

All I wish for now is I never fail you
The value's you taught me I'll teach my children too
Freed from your pain God knew no longer could
You take
I thought I knew hurt until I felt, heartbreak.

Carol Scott

Trees

Trees are great.
They stand up tall.
They give us oxygen.
But sometimes they fall.

In winter they go to sleep.
They sleep for three months,
and wake up with new
leaves.
They fall in the autumn and
blow away in the strong
breeze.

Caroline Ellen O'Dowd (10)

My Lucky Black Cat

We sit together in the firelight glow
Harmony and contentment between us flow
She's sleek and black and her green eyes gleam
They close, whiskers twitch and she begins to dream

Her paws move as if she's running fast
Do cats ever link their minds with the past?
Is she hunting or having a fight
Or with a witch on a broomstick gliding through the night

I wonder if she ever longs to be free
Is she living the life she was meant to be
The supreme grace of the cat family
Will always be a source of wonder to me

She awakens, stretches and jumps on my knee
Deep purring shows she's contented with me
The thought of more exciting places to roam
Seldom worries those who are happy at home

Her air of independence she'll never lose
She'll often do the opposite to whatever I choose
Sometimes when I'm annoyed with human company
Her expression clearly says, stay serene like me

At times when stress puts endurance to full test
A cat's attitude to life seems best
To enjoy each day be it sunshine or rain
For each passing hour will never come again

Joyce Atkinson

For Every Action There Is A Deed

And for every deed there is one less
seed
By man's every nature he is a
follower to the cause, by mans
every nature is persistence brings
destruction and wars
we are told and we listen
we are told and we accept
by is authority is honesty
and is virtuousness
for we are is seeds that help
him believe is words speak truth
in-unto- us is address.
This is moment of glory is just
another story of history in
            repeated darkness

A Williams

Seeking

Is there a light at the end of the tunnel
will the darkness ever disappear
for its presence surround me
inwardly pressing
so I nearly choke on my tears
sometimes the weight is unbearable
who can I go to
when I feel shattered, almost broken
don't anyone understand
I have experienced many pleasures
have a home, car, family
yet, I'm still disturbed deep inside
and I don't have inner peace
Lord I once walked with you
are you still there
do you really care
hang on to me in my despair.

Chris Batley

A Vision In Words

The lilting words of poetry.
Bringing scenes to life.
Spoken words that beautify.
True wonderment of life.

Poets have a vision.
Most people cannot see.
Visions of tranquillity
That's there for all to see.

Beauty and contentment
Conjured in the mind.
Just a look a little closer.
Poetic visions you will find.
Lilting words, like music.
That skip and dance in time.
Natures, natural beauty.
Put into words that rhyme.

Leslie Rushbury

Thoughts In A Railway Train

On every side are many different faces,
Some sad, some kind, some real hard cases;
And as each person at some other looks
Their thoughts are varied as a library of books.

With reading, writing some are occupied,
While some another's character deride.
Still more sit lost in meditative thought;
Their romance, failure or success to sort.

For crimes are planned, and news is made,
Money lent and debts repaid;
Fortunes won, and characters blackened,
But a lull ensues as the speed is slackened.
As one, a hundred heads emerge, demanding
The cause of the delay, while others standing
Suspect the nearing of another station;
Begin preparing luggage in anticipation.

These, and a myriad of other things take place;
Unthought of, till brought face to face
We have them laid before us and made plain
By lack of occupation, constant study in a railway train.

P T Charles

The Mystery Of A Garden

Be silent in a garden
discover the mystery there.
Under every flower
little creatures are aware.

Do you feel light hearted in a garden
like a fairy fantasy.
With fragrant smells of blossoms
isn't it heavenly.

Linger at night in a garden
after a hot summers day.
Mock orange smells so sweetly
I'm, sure you will want to stay.

Taste the fruit of a garden
strawberries senuel with cream.
Or a bowl of cherries
oh, what a lovely dream.

Step into the orchard garden
when the sun sends its golden rays.
Gathering baskets of apples
to store for old winter's days.

To end the year in the garden
when the cold is so keen.
Even now not lonely
visiting birds are seen.

Thank you Lord for your blessings
of weather earth and sky,
for the wind to scatter seedlings
while in my chair I bide

Naomi Ruth Whiting

Rocking Chair

The old woman sits in her rocking chair,
Brushing her long wispy grey hair.

She waits for someone to come,
No-one there she starts to rock and hum.

Food in her kitchen out of date milk gone bad,
The old woman rocks, confused, lonely and sad.

She sits alone in her now darkened house,
Silence is loud, except for a scurrying mouse.

Two days later . . . still no-one, the old woman still in her rocking
chair
Died, alone, 'cause people forgot she was there,
People just didn't care.

Sue Cranstone

Early Spring

The light breeze
Is highlighted
By the trees
Gently swaying . . .

Under a canopy
Of smoke coloured clouds
With a smattering
Of pinkish orange
And light blue sky.

It's mid February
And dusk approaches.

The cool wind
Is pleasant
As it caresses my face
Like an angels embrace.

This astonishingly mild February
Is very welcome indeed.
The spring flowers
Have sprung,
Contributing their mass
Of colour,
As they are tempted
By the sun . . .

To treat us all
To a wonderful show.
Whether snowdrop, crocus
Or magnificent daffodil.

Nature, the greatest show on Earth

Ian Mowatt

Gerrin' Mi Air Off!

Ah thought a'd go to college
to learn a thing or two, well . . .
at school I weren't right clever
a wer off a lot wi flu.

Mi friends said
be assertive
you've got to learn to say no
so that's what I'm doin at the moment
when I can be bothered to go.

This week, we were looking at anger
and how to manage it best,
Gill locks herself in the bedroom
and jumps up and down in her vest

Val throws plates at her husband
a punchbag works for Joyce
Moira drives to the country
and sings in a loud raucous voice

Pam stamps her feet in the parlour
and screams as loud as she can
when Arthur's anger gets to him
he drinks pints of black and tan.

Angie does the housework
polishing all but the cat
Paula sees her therapist
for a cup of tea and a chat.

Carla munches crunchie bars
Sonia punches walls
Penelope uses lavender oil
and Chinese tension balls.

117

Well, I know I said I weren't clever
but I can't be far off 't' mark
'cos when I get mi 'air' off
I just tek a walk in the park.

Sue Stridgen

A Cry For Help

I have six children it's hard to cope it's also
hard to keep the money afloat.

I once had a husband who helped me out but he
could not cope so he ran out.

So now I'm left all alone with just six
children and a house to call my own.

I sometimes cry myself to sleep and wonder how
I will make ends meet.

I've often thought to end it all but what will
happen to my children I love them all.

I've started drinking to ease the pain but my
life has stayed the same.

I've asked for help what more can I do I'll
have to stop drinking and crying will not do.

Liam Shakespeare

Our Patron Saints

St George, the saint of our land,
By your side we proudly stand;
To keep the evil from us at bay
It was the dragon you did slay.

The Irish parade on St Patrick's day.
Through the streets they march away;
With a lot of fuss they leap about;
'It's St Patrick's day' they all shout.

The Welsh all sing on St David's day;
To him a daffodil they all display.
They then all sing in full voice,
'St David was our greatest choice'.

The Scots all dance on St Andrew's day.
They drink and dance the night away;
The swirling kilt to the sound of pipes,
For them St Andrew is just right.

The English are quiet on St George's day,
Going about their business in every way,
But in their hearts there deep down
St George, their patron saint, is found.

Francis Allen

Don't Leave

How can I let you slip away
When my life will only be full of loneliness?
I don't know how you can leave me here
You know I'll only feel sadness.

Please don't leave me here, all alone
I only want to have you here, by my side
How can you do this to me
When I'll only have an unhappy time?

Please don't go, I beg you
You can't leave me here
You can't let me lie here
In all my sodden tears.

Why did you have to leave me?
I begged and pleaded with you
To stay here with me;
And now my whole life has gone, too.

How could you do this to me?
Was it all my fault?
I could never forget about you
And all you've ever done.

Don't tell me you're sorry,
You can't be now;
Don't try coming near again
You'll only make me feel more down.

Sarah L Grigor

Day Break

Drawing aside the velvet curtains of dusk,
    the rested Sun rolled his head off the black
    pillow of night and, yawning, waved away his blanket
    of wispy clouds, to reveal the blue heaven of day; then
    smiled with a warmth to make the oceans simmer, and
    sparkle jewel-like.

William G Thomas

The Lantern

If I could write I would drop you a line,
But not only is my left hand strapped up
I do wonder if my right one is mine,
Curled over like an insensible cup . . .

I need them to walk: they are my support;
Should they both fail me - as indeed they may -
Could one face a life with no last resort?
Treason of the years: what a price to pay!

Yet that is how so many have to cope;
Imagine you had no hands and no legs
Could you keep your Faith and rely on Hope?

If ever, old Friend, you reached for the dregs
Knowing that you are alone with your plight,
Seek then the Lord: His lantern is your light.

F Van Haelewyck

My Wonderful Mother

From birth you gave me love and care,
since then a special bond we share,
you are always there if I am in need,
my wonderful mother, so special indeed.

You taught me how to crawl and walk,
to drink and feed, and then how to talk,
I remember you taught me right from wrong,
at bedtime you'd read, or sing me a song.

You took me to school, on that very first day,
I cried a little, when you walked away,
after school you would be at the gate,
my wonderful mother, always there, never late.

When leaving school, life took a sudden change,
going places without you, I felt rather strange,
yet wherever I went, and the things I had done,
'twas always a pleasure, being back home with mum.

Then came the day I turned to pastures anew,
entering into Holy matrimony, when I said 'I do'
always in my thoughts, and in my daily prayer,
my wonderful mother, you will always be there.

Wenn the Penn

A Time For Everything

There is a time for sowing and a time for reaping,
a time to dream and watch the world go by,
but sometimes one should sit in contemplation
and try to fathom out the reasons why.

There is a time for mourning and a time for dancing,
a time for laughter in the midst of tears,
for in the noise and bustle of the city
one listens but one very rarely hears.

There is a time for sorrow and a time for joy,
a time to meditate and hear you call,
and in the quiet and stillness of the evening
I see your face and hear the petals fall.

There is a time to act, a time for hesitation,
a time to walk away and leave the town,
for in the midst of frenzy and frustration
the sun still rises and it still goes down.

Suzanne Low Steenson

Devotion

Such a sweet little lady sits by the bed
Of her husband, who is desperately ill
The hours pass by, without a word
Her patience is one of skill.
It's so sad, to see her, but what can I do
To help her and ease the pain
We chat and we smile but I am lost for words
As another day goes by again.
I will be her friend, then she is not alone
But it's difficult to put into words,
I am here if she needs me
And would like to help
Even when she goes home.
Her name is Margaret, she is very sweet
We were about to leave and go home,
But my husband said, give her these flowers
For she sits there all alone.

Elsie Keen

126

Somebody's There For You

Somebody is here for you in your time of need
Somebody deeply cares for you indeed
When we are down and problems rise
To us alone they are a great size
But to share a burden helps to ease
The inward pain so tight it can seize
To ease that pain this inward grief
Is to spit it out on winds of breeze
Someday soon your burden shall fly
On winds or air as it passes by
So once again you shall feel oh so free
To face once again your life full of glee

B Laverty

Wild Flowers And Sounds of Springtime

In the spring time it is fine
to be alive, I love to see the
wild flowers thrive.
Along the stream and through the
wood, they all are looking so very good.
Clusters of daffodils everywhere showing
their faces to the air.
Primroses growing along the banks
of the stream are sight that must
be seen.
The lake is enhanced by the sun
where the geese and ducks are having
fun.
Gagling and quacking everywhere
with piercing sounds that vibrate
through the air.

Timothy Shepherd Wilkie

Thine Is The Hand

Thine is the hand that fashioned the sun
The moon, and all that between them lay
The stars and the night when day is done
Cosmic diamonds sprinkled in the sky

Thine is the hand that fashioned the sea
The pebbles, the sand and rocky shore
Flowers that garland each mighty tree
Perfection, according to Thy law

Thine is the hand that fashioned mountains
Valleys, lined with every shade of green
Rainbow streams filled with sparkling fountains
More beauty this world has never seen

This self-same hand, I know, fashioned me
Gave me, gave us all, a chance to grow
To bud and to flower like a tree
To learn that we reap just what we sow

So that in time, you, yes, just like me
If we do as our God so commands
Will then be free, in eternity
To love all, as He justly demands.

Ellen E Stephenson

Tha's Our Bridge

'We've got a wrought iron structure
in the bridge at the end of our street.

My Da' says it wasn't there when he was a boy,
Cos it's where he and his friends used to meet.
So he should know.

Those stone supports come from Bath. At the ends.
Oh, Portland is it? I didn't know.
Isn't there a man called Bill there?

The Corporation don't let the ironwork rust;
not like our railings,
Which turn to flaky dust, if you pick them.

The bridge rises up in the middle, and then
It drops down again
On the other side. And so do the railings.

On Saturdays, my mates and me
run sticks across them 'cos we like the sound it makes.
Drives the shopkeepers at the ends wild.

Mam says the bridge is gracious;
but that's what me Aunty Maud calls my sister.
Da' says Mam means it's got grace,
but it don't remind me of owt to do with God.

There are lots of curves though:
It's like an arch underneath.
And there are all these patterns,
if you look from Cooper's bank.

They used to make those steel beams
down the back: near where we used to live.
My Da' used to work there
For a while, till they laid 'im off'.

When I became an Engineer,
I once revisited my past.
There's a simplicity in some structures, which
As a boy, helped me appreciate the Arts.

Philip Walker

A Thought To Make You Ponder On A Hot Summer's Day

The hippopotamus said the rhinosarus
'The brontosaurus is really a mouse!'
But the rhinosarus said to the hippopotamus
That this was 'really quite ridiculous.'

'How can it be?' asked the rhinosarus to the hippopotamus
'That the brontosaurus is a mouse,
When it is quite clear that the brontosaurus
Is bigger than the biggest house?'

'Ah' said the hippopotamus to the rhinosarus,
'But if you stand the brontosaurus against the universe,
He would surely look like a mouse,
And certainly more petite than a house!'

'I beg to differ' said the rhinosarus to the hippopotamus.
'If using such a great contrast my fine chap,
Then surely the brontosaurus would be more of an ant,
Than a mouse or a house perhaps?'

'Hmm' thought the hippopotamus and 'Hmm' he thought again,
For this was truly more complex a thought
Then he had stored in his brain.
He turned to the rhinosarus and exclaimed.

'Enough I say, enough of all this,
For this is truly beginning to be a bore.
I only meant it don't you know in jest,
But you insist on making it more of a chore.'

'Oh my word' gasped the rhinosarus to the hippopotamus,
'It was you who started this ridiculous hypothesis,
And I mean this quite sincerely hippopotamus
That a brontosaurus is a brontosaurus is a brontosaurus.'

And with this, the hippopotamus turned with a grunt.
Extremely annoyed at his supposed friend rhinosarus
He still believed in his theory about the brontosaurus,
Who was obviously and unmistakably a mouse, a mouse, a mouse.

Nicola Sivyer

Forget Me Not!

Passing along a road one day,
As I continued on my way,
By a wall, saw a patch of blue,
Bringing back memories of you!
Those forget-me-nots, small and gay,
Gave thoughts of how you showed the way,
How could I ever forget you!
Showing me the way, clear and true.
Telling of a Saviours great love,
Leaving for us, His home above,
Living, then dying, for us all,
Not turning away those who call.
Through you I learnt to love Him too,
So I could never forget you!

Lilian M Loftus

134

My Mother

You have always been a rock for me
In this world's shifting sand.
You're someone I can turn to
When I need a helping hand.

You have always been my anchor
In the stormy sea of life.
You're always there when I need someone
In sickness or in strife!

You think of me before yourself.
You always ease my pain.
You never say 'I told you so!'
You're sunshine, after rain!

I know I can rely on you
To always see things through.
You are my shelter from the wind.
I can always trust in you!

Den Evans

Granda

In the silence of night as I lie in
my bed,
Pictures of Granda appear in
my head;
His wrinkled old face, his eyes,
his smile.
How much I love Granda, so caring
and kind.
Sometimes I think of when Granda is
gone,
I will kneel by his bed and think
memories fond,
Those pictures of him will appear in
my head,
And I'll cry loving tears as I kneel
by his bed.
Granda, I love you, and you love
me too,
In heaven we'll meet again, just me
and you.
I think of memories fond that I always
will keep,
Then I shut my eyes tight and
fall gently asleep.

Jennie Jacques

Mother's Love

A mother's love goes so deep
She often, sits, thinks and weeps
Will her children ever know
How deep their mother's feelings go.

Will they ever sit down too
and remember all the things, Mums do,
The worry, guilt and the pain
Will they ever feel the same

Love your Mum while she's here
Be grateful you have her near
When she's gone it's much too late
There is no time to harbour hate.

So much to do, so little time
If only I'd read you one more rhyme
I tried to give you all I could
There were times, when things were good

It was not easy to let you go
Scold you, or just say . . . no
If only you could understand,
And not dismiss me 'out of hand'.

A Mother's love is entire and true
You're in her thoughts, whatever you do
Wherever you go, She is always there
Never Again Will You Have Such Care.

Elizabeth Ann Driver

Remember Wildlife

Through the high branches of beech, shines the cool autumn sun.
Beneath, amongst brown leaves and nut husks, squirrels are having
fun.
Songbirds seem to be mourning the passing of summer bliss.
Raising their voices, against the beginning of cold winter winds kiss.

Animals prepare for freezing winter days and nights.
Each changing lifestyles and habits, within their own rights.
Humans pass by, oblivious to changes gone unseen
To them all winter means is a frozen screen.

Not for them, digging in, and storing up of food.
Or burrowing down a warm pit, in hibernation mood.
We take our lives for granted, and wrap up from the cold.
And go to local supermarkets, where our food is sold.

Just remember next year, when cold winds start to blow.
And birds around your garden, have nowhere else to go.
The little furry animals, can find no food to eat,
Put food out in your garden, and give them all a treat.

J R Hall

Winter's Realm

The night is cold,
My fire is burning bright,
The wind is whistling
Round the eaves,
And the snowflakes
Fall all night.
We wake up
In the morning
To a silent, sullen day,
Where underneath
A leaden sky
More snow is on the way.
And in the valley
Far below,
I hear the
Church bells ring,
And huddle closer
To the fire,
And say a prayer -
For Spring.

V B D'Wit